SONATA in G minor, Op.49 No.1

The detailed analysis in *A Companion to Beethoven's Pianoforte Sonatas** deals with many matters of rhythm and melody that concern the player. The sonatas of Op.49 will be given to very young players; but no player is too young to learn music as musical sense and not as a mere mass of finger exercises.

Andante

Bars 1–4 As a finger-exercise the l.h. of these bars is both difficult and interesting. There is pleasure in the task of getting these 3rds to flow smoothly, with firm fingers and a loose wrist. Mark the normal accents as well as Beethoven's *mfp* – that is to say, do not let the 2nd and 4th of the bar become as strong as the 1st and 3rd. (The tempo is, of course, a flowing 4-in-the-bar rather than a 2.)

Several fingerings are possible, but it is always best to take repeated notes with a change of finger, as in the case of the repeated F♯ and B♮ – especially as these belong to different voices. When you have mastered this passage so that it sings in the upper and lower notes alike, you will have learnt something that will be always turning up in fine music. Do not stiffen or squirm, but take the least possible movement from each note to the next. Gaps matter far less than inequalities of tone. When your tone is smooth and your accents natural, any gaps you have been compelled to make will soon vanish, whereas your legato might stand all the tests of mechanical clicking instruments, or even of organ-playing, and yet sound like stumbling over a ploughed field if your tone is unequal.

The very precise mark *mfp* is characteristic of Mozart, and it is strange that Beethoven did not keep it in use in later works.

b.14 Grace-notes fall on the beat. This delays the main note, but the delay will not be noticed if the main note receives its proper accent. If the grace-notes come too soon they spoil the previous note.

b.17 Turns over a dot fall, as it were, on the dot. Do not let them become stiff. Think of ♪♪♪♪♪ 𝅘𝅥 rather than of ♪♪♪♪♪ 𝅘𝅥 though probably the latter is what the arithmetic of the case will come to. It is mainly a question of accent. One secret of good ornaments is that they have a much lighter tone than the main notes.

bb.33/34–35 A shake that starts a new passage had better begin on the main note. But when the main note has just been struck the shake will begin on the upper note. Most shakes will be supposed to end with turns if the next note rises; but if it falls to the note immediately below, it had better be without turn. Thus these bars will work out

Practise this carefully, getting the left hand as strong and steady as the right (with separate practice) and keeping your quavers as large as will make room for your ornaments. That is to say, so long as your ornaments need to be practised slowly your quavers must be kept in proportion to them just as much as when you are playing in tempo. Always play *in time*, however remote the prospect of playing *in tempo* may be.

It is much better to learn the [...] ments than merely to have the e[...]s view written down in place of the composer's notation.

bb.43–44 Short grace-notes.

b.64 The *piano* D enters as if it had intended to rise an octave like the previous sequence, but it is checked by the discovery that it is the first note of the main theme. It implies something like a *crescendo* before it. It should arrive punctually, but you may then give it a very slight extra moment in which it can, as it were, look round and make up its mind to fall (quite legato) into the theme.

bb.71/72 ff. The fact that the theme is in the left hand should not make you neglect the beautiful counterpoint of the right. Do not, however, fall into the opposite mistake of putting a leaden quaver outline into it in bb.72, 74, 76 and 77. Beethoven always tells us when he wants notes to be held down, and he has no positive sign for telling us the contrary; so we must never be officious and hold down notes that he has left unencumbered.

b.88 Note that this turn is not over the dot but over the semiquaver. It therefore means ♩. ♬♬

bb.99, 101 Let these echoes of the bass theme arise quietly out of the monotoned chords without disturbing their flow.

b.103 Do not make crotchets of the top notes. When Haydn writes passages of this kind for strings he is so far from desiring any such effect that he will make two violins meet on the *bottom* notes, as in the Adagio of the Quartet Op.64 No.4.

Rondo: *Allegro*

At a later period Beethoven would certainly have called this an *allegretto*. It is very important to make quite clear to the listener that the main accents of the delightful first theme come on the groups 𝄞 and 𝄞 Already in the third full bar a *sforzando* outweighs the main accent, so that if this is not clearly established before and after we shall fail to appreciate the lilt. Beethoven here intelligently anticipates the *Blue Danube* Waltz, the rhythm of which will always be misunderstood if the bass is not well marked and brought in at the right moment, *i.e.* at the *second* bar.

Bar 4 The l.h. crotchet will have to give way to r.h., and cannot therefore be longer than a quaver. But if Beethoven had written it as a quaver every player would have cut it too short.

bb.9–12 The sonatas of Op.49 were written in 1796, and published in 1805 without Beethoven's permission. We therefore cannot rely on the phrasing being complete, and may rather be surprised that it is in such good order. So if you like to take this figure as ♪♪♩ there is nothing to prevent you. But it is at least equally good with all the notes detached.

* *A Companion to Beethoven's Pianoforte Sonatas: A Complete Book of Analyses.* (Associated Board)

b.16   The episode in the minor begins with the *forte* of this bar; and the slightly confused paragraphs become clearer if we take from the middle of 16 to 23 as a continuous phrase.

bb.20–25   The bracketed marks are imported from the parallel passage 68–73, where they are authentic.

b.32   The new tune begins with this bar. A curious feature of the rhythm is that b.40 is the eighth of the paragraph, and that in repeating itself from this point the rhythmic sense of the tune is changed, so that 41 is the first bar of the phrase, though it corresponds to 33 which was the second bar of the phrase.

The accompaniment is better detached than phrased thus ♪♪♩ ; though that phrasing is also possible.

b.48   The l.h. arpeggio leads up to r.h., and the melody should arise straight out of it.

b.55   Do not let the turn be stiff. ♪♪♪♪♪ is better than ♩ ♪♪♪♪

bb.96–99   Do not miss the point of this dialogue between l.h. and r.h. A *crescendo* will do no harm, though Beethoven has not indicated it.

b.137   The left hand is now, as in 96–99, a complete personage on equal terms with the right.

bb.145–146   The l.h. detached dominant belongs to the figure of r.h., thus [musical example] etc.

b.163   Let the *ff* be quite sudden. A *diminuendo* would be better than any *crescendo* to lead up to it.

DONALD FRANCIS TOVEY

SONATA
in G minor

BEETHOVEN, Op. 49. No.1

(see notes)

RONDO
Allegro

Printed in England by Calligraving Limited Thetford Norfolk

A.B.250

5:01